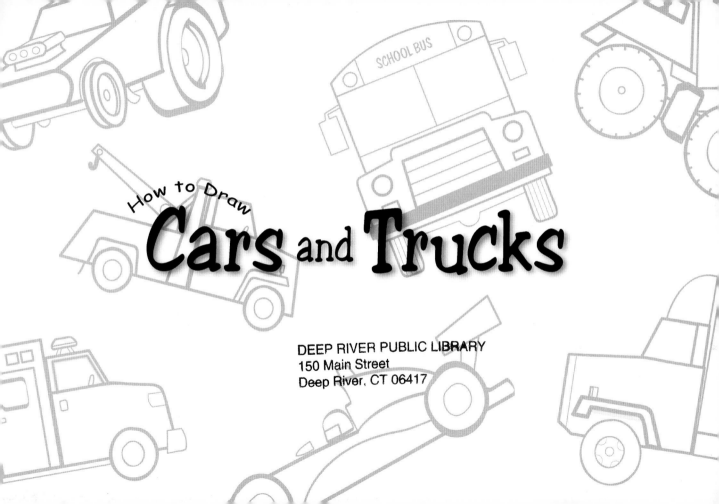

How to Draw

Cars and Trucks

For Jesse, Jasmine, Justin, Jordan, Melina, and Matthew

Published in the United States of America by The Child's World®
PO Box 326 • Chanhassen, MN 55317-0326
800-599-READ • www.childsworld.com

Acknowledgments
Illustration and Design: Rob Court
Production: The Creative Spark, San Juan Capistrano, CA

Registration

Library of Congress Cataloging-in-Publication Data
Court, Rob, 1956–
  How to draw cars and trucks / by Rob Court.
    p. cm. — (Doodle books)
  ISBN-13: 978-1-59296-804-6 (library bound : alk. paper)
  ISBN-10: 1-59296-804-X (library bound : alk. paper)
  1. Automobiles in art—Juvenile literature. 2. Trucks in art—Juvenile
literature. 3. Drawing—Technique—Juvenile literature. I. Title. II. Series.

NC825.A8C68 2007
743'.8962922—dc22
                                    2006031558

The Scribbles Institute™

How to Draw
Cars and Trucks

by Rob Court

The Child's World

sports car

1

2

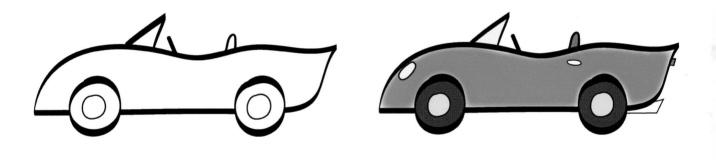

3

4

small car

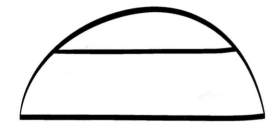

1

2

4

tow truck

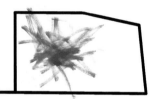

1

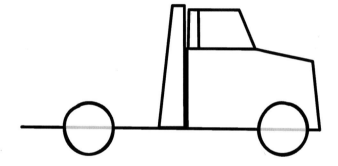

 2

3

4

limousine

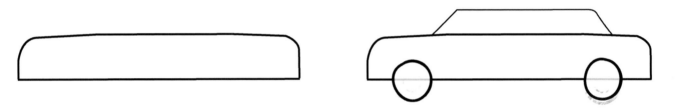

1

2

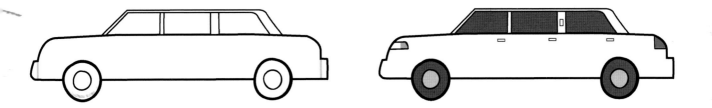

3

4

dump truck

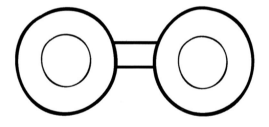

1

2

3

4

cement truck

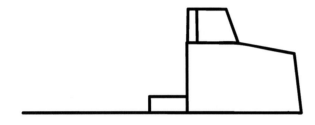

1

2

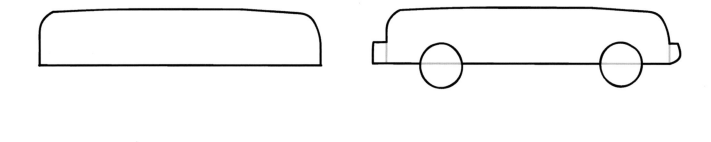

1

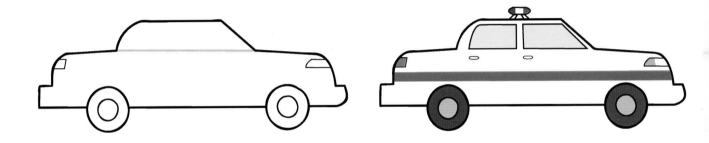

3

4

fire truck

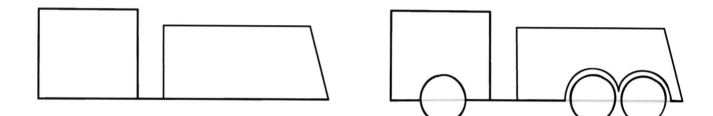

2

3

4

delivery truck

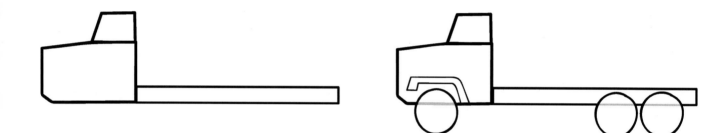

1

2

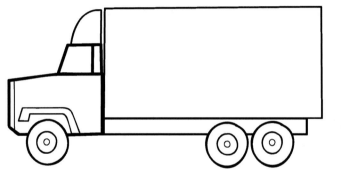

3

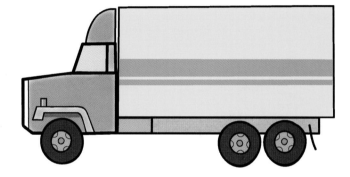

4

race car

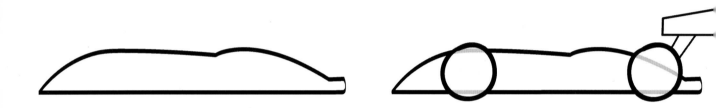

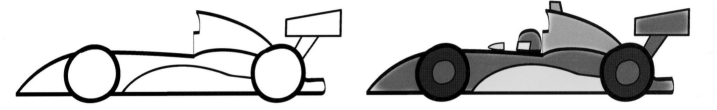

3

4

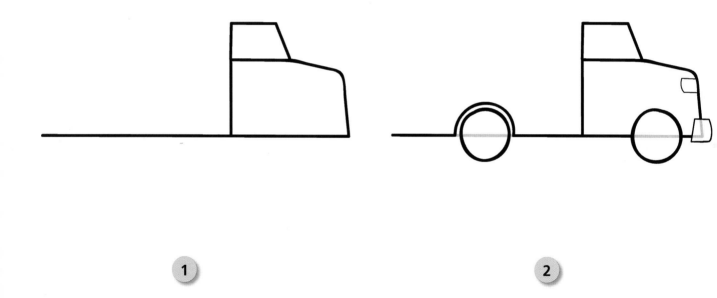

1

2

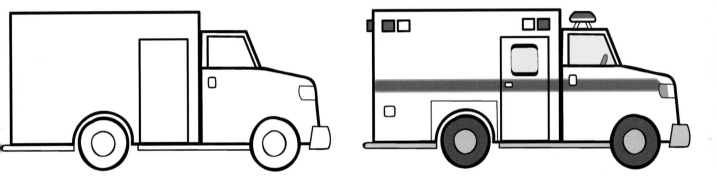

3

4

school bus

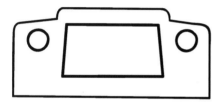

1

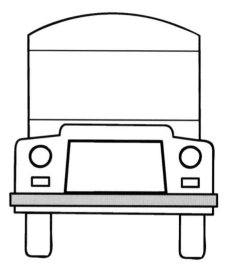

2

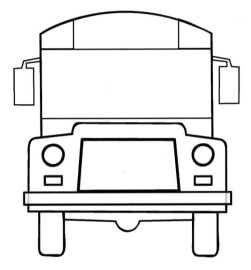

3

4

monster truck

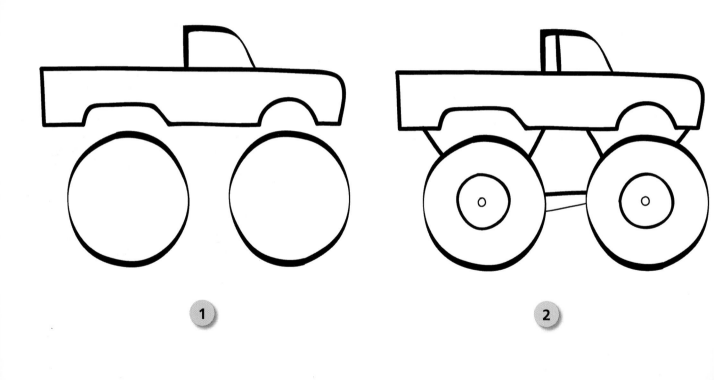

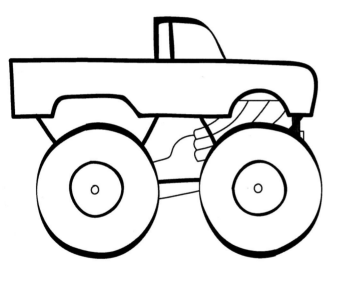

3

4

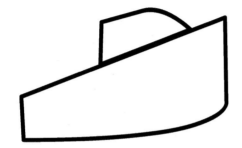

1

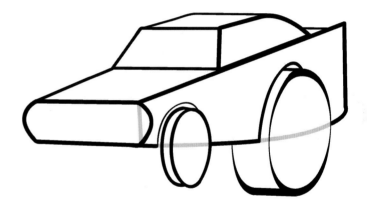

2

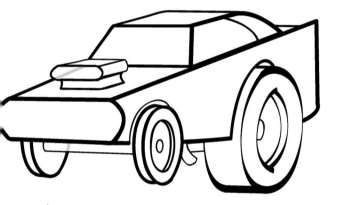

3

4

lines

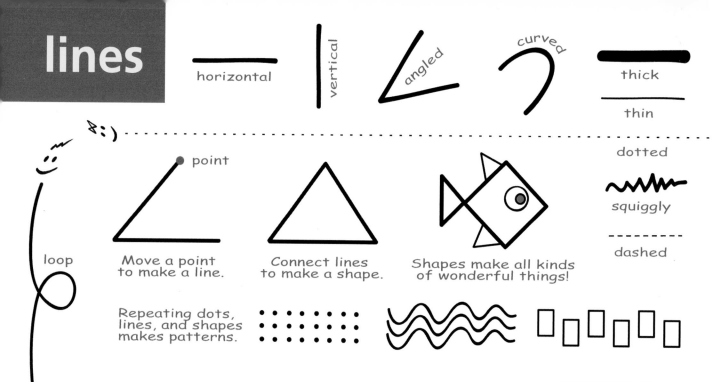

horizontal

vertical

angled

curved

thick

thin

point

dotted

squiggly

dashed

loop

Move a point to make a line.

Connect lines to make a shape.

Shapes make all kinds of wonderful things!

Repeating dots, lines, and shapes makes patterns.

About the Author

Rob Court is a graphic artist and illustrator. He started the Scribbles Institute to help students, parents, and teachers learn about drawing and visual art. Please visit www.scribblesinstitute.com